SUBMIT, RESIST, FLEE:

Strategies to Living a Victorious Life

SUBMIT, RESIST, FLEE:

Strategies to Living a Victorious Life

ROSZIEN KAY LEWIS

CONFESSIONS PUBLISHING

Scripture quotations marked (NLT) are taken from the *Holy Bible*, New Living Translation © 2004. Wheaton, Ill: Tyndale House Publisher.

Scripture quotations marked (KJV) are taken from the *Holy Bible*, King James Version.

Scripture quotations marked (ESV) are taken from the *Holy Bible*, English Standard Version © 2001 by Crossway Bibles, a division of Good News Publishers. Used by permission. All rights reserved.

Scripture quotations marked (NIV) are taken from the *Holy Bible*, New International Version. Zondervan Publishing House © 1984. Used by permission. All rights reserved.

Scripture quotations marked (NKJV) are taken from the *Holy Bible*, New King James Version © 1982 by Thomas Nelson. Used by permission. All rights reserved.

Submit, Resist, Flee: Strategies To Living A Victorious Life

Copyright © 2020 Roszien Kay Lewis

ISBN: 978-1-7359620-2-3

Printed and bound in the United States of America.

All Rights Reserved. No part of this publication may be reproduced, stored in a retrieval system, or transmitted, in any form or by any means- electronic, mechanical, photocopying, recording, or otherwise- used in any manner whatsoever without the express written permission of the author, Roszien Kay Lewis.

Editor: Erick Markley

CONFESSIONS PUBLISHING

Confessions Publishing is a subsidiary of Roszien Kay LLC, Lancaster, CA 93536

For information regarding discounts on bulk purchase and all other inquiries, please contact the author directly at roszien@gmail.com

AUTHOR'S OTHER BOOKS

Confessions of An Overcomer: From Tragedy to Triumph

Confessions of An Overcomer: The Truth About the Wait

Getting Spiritually Snatched

Surrender: Surrendering It All To Gain It All

Hidden Preparation

The Wilderness

CONTENTS

INTRODUCTION	9
SUBMIT	15
RESIST	33
FLEE	81
THE IMPORTANCE OF PRAYER	85
THOSE WHO SUBMITTED AND RESISTED	91
CONCLUSION	105

INTRODUCTION

INTRODUCTION

As humans we'll exert great effort as we try many different ways to arrive at a desired solution, to obtain a desired result, or to reach a desired conclusion. This approach is something that has been placed inside of us from the time that we were children. When faced with difficulties as a child, our parents, or other adults, cheered us on when we would try many different ways to solve something. Because of its success on a number of occasions, though we had plenty of failures, we've carried this approach over into adulthood.

Now as adults, when faced with difficult or trying situations, we are open to doing as many different things as possible to reach a desired end. Honestly, we often select the ways and solutions that are easier, more comfortable, and less time consuming, if it means that we get what we want regardless of the consequences at times.

Although this approach is great for the majority of situations, and works in many instances of our lives, this approach isn't going to work when our desire, goal, and aim is to achieve something spiritually. No matter how intelligent we are, how many corners we cut, or how many different approaches our finite minds may come up with, there are certain things that must be done exactly God's way!

Our efforts, systems, and approaches are futile when they aren't done according to the Lord's desires or instructions. It doesn't matter how much knowledge we have obtained about a matter either. It doesn't matter how successful we may appear to be in our way of approaching something on our spiritual journey either. It's still inefficient if it is contrary to what God instructs and desires. God's knowledge trumps ours because His thoughts and ways are far above ours. They take into consideration what we don't know or cannot see or sense.

Therefore, if we are to be successful on our journey of spiritual growth and maturity, one must accept the fact that certain things must be done God's way and His way only.

One area that this applies to is resisting our adversary. When caught face to face with temptation and/or attacks, we must strictly follow the instructions given in James 4:7 (KJV), *"Submit yourselves therefore to God. Resist the devil, and he will*

INTRODUCTION

flee from you." Without following these instructions, we are likely to find ourselves on the wrong side of the battle: defeat.

The information in the proceeding pages is aimed at equipping you with what's needed, not only for you to understand what is required by James 4:7, but it's aimed at teaching you how to live a victorious life, despite the adversary's attacks!

SUBMIT

I

SUBMIT

"Submit yourselves therefore to God . . ."
(James 4:7)

According to the dictionary, to submit means, "to give over or yield to the power or authority of another. To subject to some kind of treatment or influence." The KJV dictionary goes a little further by stating that to submit means, "to surrender; to yield one's person to the power of another; to give up resistance."

Typically, true submission is done voluntarily and freely. It's not forced or obtained from someone by manipulation. The submission that God requires is beyond yielding oneself merely to His commands which are stated in His Word. Rather, there is an expectation that when we submit to Him, we become humble; there should be a sense of weakness and emptiness, and an understanding that we are in need of His grace.

As much as we strive to submit to the Lord, there are times when we experience difficulty—no matter how good our intentions may be. Oftentimes, we start off with so much zeal, obeying the Lord effortlessly. Then, all of a sudden, we get caught off guard by an attack from the enemy and then start to doubt God, and experience moments of uncertainty. If not properly checked, these moments can quickly turn into moments of difficulty, and can perhaps even spiral into moments of utter failure, which leads to our refusal to submit to God.

The reason why this occurs is because there is always a war being waged between our spirit (the part that received salvation) and our flesh (the part of us that does not want to submit to God and lacks the ability to submit to God). When our minds are not set on pleasing and submitting to God but are set on pleasing and submitting to our flesh, we become prey to the enemy each and every time. Which results in us giving into temptations, leading to our defeat.

According to Matthew 26:41 (NLT), "keep watch and pray, so that you will not give in to temptation. For the spirit is willing, but the body is weak!" The enemy (our adversary, the devil) is always watching us for an opportunity to come into our lives and cause us to become unsubmissive to the Lord. He does this by presenting different temptations to us. He does this because he knows that if we decide to give in to our flesh, he can carry us away from God, and into the hands of defeat.

To properly understand how believers can still become defeated by the enemy when they have received salvation, there must be a clear understanding of the composition of the human body. And how the enemy takes advantage of certain parts of us.

WHAT HUMANS ARE COMPRISED OF

Humans consist of three parts: the body (flesh), the soul, and the spirit. These three parts of a person makeup who we are. Through these three parts, we are able to live and interact with God and His creation.

1 Thessalonians 5:23, "And the very God of peace sanctify you wholly; and I pray God your whole Spirit and soul and body be preserved blameless unto the coming of our Lord Jesus Christ."

THE BODY

The body is the physical part of a person. It is commonly referred to as our flesh. The body is composed of the senses: sight, smell, hearing, taste, and touch. The flesh is the area of us that the enemy tempts and attacks the most. The flesh is the part of a person that does not receive salvation. It's the part of us that we must continuously crucify and bring under the subjection of Jesus Christ. Failure on our part to turn away from being led by the flesh will result in death because there is no good thing that lies within the flesh.

Romans 8:8 (KJV), "So then, they that are in the flesh cannot please God."

Galatians 5:19-21, " When you follow the desires of your sinful nature, the results are very clear: sexual immorality, impurity, lustful pleasures, idolatry, sorcery, hostility, quarreling, jealousy, outbursts of anger, selfish ambition, dissension, division, envy, drunkenness, wild parties, and other sins like these. Let me tell you again, as I have before, that anyone living that sort of life will not inherit the Kingdom of God."

Galatians 5:24 (ESV), "And those who belong to Chrsit Jesus have crucified the flesh with its passions and desires."

SUBMIT

Galatians 5:15 (KJV), "This I say then, walk in the Spirit, and ye shall not fulfill the lust of the flesh."

Romans 7:18 (ESV), "For I know that nothing good dwells in me, that is, in my flesh. For I have the desire to do what is right, but not the ability to carry it out."

Romans 8:6 (ESV), "For to set the mind on the flesh is death . . ."

Romans 8:7 (ESV), "For the mind that is set on the flesh is hostile to God, for it does not submit to God's law; indeed, it cannot."

Romans 8:5(ESV), "For those who live according to the flesh set their minds on the things of the flesh . . . "

Romans 8:13 (ESV), "For if you live according to the flesh you will die . . ."

Romans 6:16 (ESV), "Do you not know that if you present yourselves to anyone as obedient slaves, you are slaves to the one whom you obey, either of sin, which leads to death, or of obedience, which leads to righteousness?"

1 John 2:16 (ESV), "For all that is in the world—the desires of the flesh and the desires of the eyes and pride in possessions—is not from the Father but is from the world."

THE SPIRIT

The spirit of a man is the part that connects or refuses to connect to God. Our spirit relates to His Spirit, either accepting His prompting and convictions, which proves that we belong to Him, or it resists Him, proving that we don't have His Spirit. When the spirit of a man refuses to connect to God, it's connected to the adversary. When the spirit of a man is connected to the devil, it is dead.

1 Corinthians 2:14 (NKJV), "But the natural man does not receive the things of the Spirit of God, for they are foolishness to him; nor can he know them, because they are spiritually discerned."

Colossians 2:13 (NLT), You were dead because of your sins and because your sinful nature was not yet cut away. Then God made you alive with Christ, for he forgave all our sins."

Those who are spiritually dead are those who are unsubmitted and do not live for God. They see the things of God as being foolish because of their spiritually dead conditions. Those who are spiritually dead, don't have the ability to discern the things of the spirit either.

Acts 7:51(NKJV), "You stiff-necked and uncircumcised in heart and ears! You always resist the Holy Spirit; as your fathers did, so do you."

1John 2:6 (NLT), "Those who say they live in God should live their lives as Jesus did."

The spirit of a man is the part of man that interacts with God and the spiritual realm. The spirit is the part of a believer that responds to the things that come from the Spirit of God. It's the part that can understand and discern God and spiritual matters. The spirit is the part that is able to worship Him.

John 4: 24 (KJV), "God is a Spirit; and they that worship him must worship him in spirit and in truth."

Romans 8:6 (NKJV), "...but to be spiritually minded is life and peace."

Romans 8:14 (NLT), "For all who are led by the Spirit of God are children of God."

Roman 8:16 (NKJV), "The Spirit Himself bears witness with our spirit that we are children of God."

THE SOUL

The human being who is in an unrepentant state has a sinful nature, and the soul is tainted with sin. The soul is the psychological part of a person that consists of the mind, emotions, and the will. The soul is the center of many spiritual and emotional experiences.

Ezekiel 18:4 (NKJV), "Behold, all souls are Mine; the soul of the father as well as the soul of the son is Mine; The soul who sins shall die."

Matthew 22:37 (ESV), "And he said to him, "You shall love the Lord your God with all your heart and with all your soul and with all your mind."

Ezekiel 18:20 (ESV), "The soul who sins shall die . . ."

Psalm 23:3 (ESV) "He restores my soul. He leads me in paths of righteousness for his name's sake."

WHY IS THERE A STRUGGLE TO SUBMIT TO GOD?

When Adam and Eve were created, they were created in the image and likeness of God. They were pure and innocent and had no issue with submitting to God because that's all they knew. However, when Adam and Eve decided that they were going to disobey God by eating from the tree of the knowledge of good and evil after being enticed by the serpent, sin entered into them. This resulted in them dying spiritually, although they were still alive physically because their soul remained. With this death, their bodies became corrupted.

Now with the spirit being dead, their soul could only function through their sinful bodies. As a result, their bodies were only able to produce sin and death. According to Genesis 5:3 (NLT), "When Adam was 130 years old, he became the father of a son who was just like him—in his very image. He named his son Seth." This meant that not only was Adam and Eve's nature changed, but the nature of mankind was changed as well.

God, knowing that humans were now left with a soul and body that could not do anything to please Him, even if it had a desire to, promised that he would give His people a new spirit. This new Spirit would dwell within mankind and assist in helping us to turn away from our flesh and once again please God.

Ezekiel 36:26 (NKJV), "I will give you a new heart and put a new spirit within you; I will take the heart of stone out of your flesh and give you a heart of flesh."

1 Corinthians 3:16 (ESV), "Do you not know that you are God's temple and that God's Spirit dwells in you?"

SUBMIT

1 Corinthians 6: 19 (ESV), "Or do you not know that your body is a temple of the Holy Spirit within you, whom you have from God? You are not your own,"

Once a person believes in Jesus Christ for eternal life (this is a function of the soul), the person goes through the process of regeneration. According to the KJV dictionary, "regenerate" means, "reproduced; born anew; renovated in heart; changed from a natural to a spiritual state." When a person accepts Jesus Christ as their Lord and Savior, God brings the new believer to new life. This new life means that the person is now "born again" from the previous sinful state that lacked the ability to live for, understand, and obey God. There is a literal renewing and restoration of that person from the previous sinful doomed state.

2 Corinthians 5:17 (NLT), "This means that anyone who belongs to Christ has become a new person. The old life is gone; a new life has begun!"

When the Holy Spirit comes into the life of a believer, it replaces the old, dead, disobedient spirit of the person. It regenerates and lives within the believer; He baptizes them and seals them. When this occurs, the believer is now able to understand the things of God. Then and only then can the believer comprehend the Spirit of God. This means that the things of God no longer seem foolish to them.

Now, as a result of regeneration, the believer is capable of making a choice between doing right and pleasing God or doing wrong and pleasing the flesh.

THE STRUGGLE WITH SUBMISSION

Once regeneration has occurred within a believer, there is now the ability to decide whether or not one will submit to the desires of God or the desires of one's flesh. As much as the believer desires to submit to God because of their spirit being willing, it's not always easy. Remember, when one receives salvation, their spirit is saved but the flesh isn't. As a result, "[t]he sinful nature wants to do evil, which is just the opposite of what the Spirit wants. And the Spirit gives us desires that are opposite of what the sinful nature desires. These two forces are constantly fighting each other, so you are not free to carry out your good intentions" (Galatians 5:17 NLT).

The believer is in a constant inward struggle! This struggle is described perfectly below by Apostle Paul in Romans 7:14-24 (NLT):

"14 For the trouble is not with the law, for it is spiritual and good. The trouble is with me, for I am all too human, a slave to sin. 15 I don't really understand myself, for I want to do what is right, but I don't do it. Instead, I do what I hate. 16 But if I know that what I am doing wrong, this shows that I agree that the law is good. 17 So I am not the one doing wrong; it is sin living in me that does it. 18 And I know that nothing good lives in me, that is, in my sinful nature. I want to do what is right, but I can't. 19 I want to do what is good, but I don't. I don't want to do what is wrong, but I do it anyway. 20 But if I do what I don't want to do, I am not really the one doing wrong; it is sin living in me that does it. 21 I have discovered this principle of life—that when I want to do what is right, I inevitably do what is wrong. 22 I love God's law with all my heart. 23 But there is another power within me that is at war with my mind. This power makes me a slave to sin that is still within me. 24 Oh, what a miserable person I am! Who will free me from this life that is dominated by sin and death?"

It's clear to see from Apostle Paul's own admission that the struggle is real! He was a man that had been completely devoted and committed to Jesus Christ from the moment that he encountered Christ on the road to Damascus. He was a man that loved and lived the word of God to the point that he was used by the Holy Spirit to write ⅔ of the New Testament. And yet he too experienced the inward struggle.

This shows that it doesn't matter how many scriptures one rehearses, memorizes, and lives, there will still be a struggle going on within one's flesh. A struggle that directly impacts our submission to God.

HOW TO SUBMIT TO GOD

Although we cannot avoid the inward struggle that impacts our submission to God, we must still strive to submit to Him anyways. The way in which we do this is by obeying the leading, guiding, and prompting of the Holy Spirit. The Holy Spirit is the one who knows the mind of God. Therefore, He is the only one capable of directing and showing us God's will for our lives. Aside from following the leading and guiding of the Holy Spirit, we submit to God by obeying His written Word and humbling ourselves.

If you'd recall, our spirit is the part of us that either connects to God or refuses to connect to God. The more we allow the Holy Spirit to lead us, the more likely we are to submit to Him. The more we practice submitting to God, the easier it becomes. The easier it becomes to submit to God in our daily lives, the more it will become commonplace.

Submission is a process. As we make daily choices to humble ourselves and obey God, we become stronger and more able to submit. As we continue on our journey of submission, we are transformed into the image of Christ. This transformation, or the process of it, is something that will continue until the day of Jesus Christ. As Apostle Paul stated in 2 Corinthians 3:18, "But we all, with unveiled face beholding as in a mirror the glory of the Lord, are changed into the same image from glory to glory even as by the Spirit of the Lord."

Philippians 1:6 (NLT), "And I am certain that God, who begun the good work within you, will continue his work until it is finally finished on the day when Christ Jesus returns."

SUBMISSION IS GOD'S DESIRE FOR US

God desires for us to submit to Him because He is a loving Father that knows what's best for us. He is our Creator. He created each and every one of us for a purpose. A purpose that we cannot reach without following His plan through submission.

We cannot know the path that He has designed for us to walk down without submitting to His will, authority, and plan for our individual lives. We cannot be properly prepared for the attacks of the enemy if we are unwilling to submit to God!

God is the Alpha and the Omega, the beginning and the end. He's everywhere at the same time. He knows everything that is happening and will happen on earth. This knowing includes every battle that the enemy has planned to launch against you!

RESIST

II
RESIST

"Resist the devil..."
(James 4:7)

James tells believers in James 4:7 to, "resist the devil." According to the KJV dictionary, to resist means, "to stand against; to withstand, to act in opposition, or to oppose... to strive against; to endeavor to counteract, defeat or frustrate. To baffle, to disappoint."

In telling the early church this, James recognized that they needed to know what to do when the enemy came up against them. He knew that there would come a time in their lives, as well as in ours, when we would have to withstand the attacks of the enemy.

As mentioned in the previous chapter, one must first submit to God if they are to be successful in counteracting, defeating, or frustrating the enemy. Without submission to God, one cannot resist the enemy. Without the power of God, one cannot resist the enemy and those who make up the kingdom of darkness, because standing alone, humans are not equipped or strong enough to do so.

The kingdom of darkness is a force to be reckoned with for humans. Although many try to ignore its existence, that doesn't negate the fact that it is real. According to Ephesians 6:12 (ESV), *"For we are not fighting against flesh-and-blood enemies, but against evil rulers and authorities of the unseen world, against mighty powers in this dark world, and against evil spirits in the heavenly places."* The devil does not come to play fair either, he comes to, ". . .steal, and to kill, and to destroy." Their sole objective (those evil spirits that make up the kingdom of darkness) is to destroy you and everything and anyone connected to you, when they have the permission to (I'll explain this in more detail later). It is only when you decide to connect yourselves to God and obey the leading of the Holy Spirit that you are able to stand against and defeat the kingdom of darkness.

I. THE KINGDOM OF DARKNESS, MANKIND, AND HOLY SPIRIT

As mentioned above, standing alone, humans are incapable of contending with, frustrating, or defeating the enemy. And it doesn't matter how strong, big, or smart we are. We cannot triumph without the power of the Holy Spirit.

To truly understand how this is even possible, we must take a look at the power humans possess, the power the kingdom of darkness possesses, and the power the Holy Spirit possesses. As well as how humans obtain the power needed to resist the enemy.

A. THE ENEMY'S POWER

Satan (also referred to as the devil and the adversary) is the enemy and opponent of those who follow God. However, it was not always like that. Satan had been blameless in all that he did from the day he was created until the day God found evil in him (Ezekiel 28:15). It wasn't until pride entered into his heart that it resulted in him devising a plan to have a throne above God. You read correctly, something God created desired to be above Him so much that he devised an entire plan.

Ezekiel 28:12-14 (NLT), "...You were the model of perfection, full of wisdom and exquisite in beauty. 13 You were in Eden, the garden of God. Your clothing was adorned with every precious stone --- red carnelian, pale-green peridot, white moonstone, blue-green beryl, onyx, green jasper, blue lapis lazuli, turquoise, and emerald --- all beautifully crafted for you and set in the finest gold. They were given to you on the day you were created. 14 I ordained and anointed you as the mighty angelic guardian. You had access to the holy mountain of God and walked among the stones of fire."

Isaiah 14:12-17 (NLT), "How you are fallen from heaven, O shining star, son of the morning! You have been thrown down to the earth, you who destroyed the nations of the world. 13 For you said to yourself, 'I will ascend to heaven and set my throne above God's stars. I will preside on the mountain of the gods far away in the north. 14 I will climb to the highest heavens and be like the Most High.' 15 Instead, you will be brought down to the place of the dead, down to its lowest depths. 16 Everyone there will stare at you and ask, 'Can this be the one who shook the earth and made the kingdom of the world tremble? 17 Is this the one who destroyed the world and made it into a wasteland? Is this the king who demolished the world's greatest cities and had no mercy on his prisoners?'"

Luke 10:18 (NKJV), "And He said to them, "I was watching Satan fall from heaven like lightning."

Revelation 12:7-9 (NLT), "Then there was war in heaven. Michael and his angels fought against the dragon and his angels. 8 And the dragon lost the battle, and he and his angels were forced out of heaven. 9 This great dragon—the ancient serpent called the devil, or Satan, the one deceiving the whole world—was thrown down to the earth with all his angels."

As you can see from the above passages of scripture, Satan was kicked out of heaven. However, he was not stripped of the power that he had been created with as a cherub, the highest created angel. Rather, when he was banished from Heaven, he became the ruler of this world and the prince of the power of the air. This means that he, and his angels who were cast out as well, are roaming the earth awaiting the day of final judgment when they will be cast into hell.

Job 1:6-7(NLT), "One day the members of the heavenly court came to present themselves before the Lord, and the Accuser, Satan, came with them. 7 "Where have you come from?" the

Lord asked Satan. Satan answered the Lord, "I have been patrolling the earth, watching everything that's going on."

Matthew 25:41 (NKJV), "Then He will also say to those on the left hand, 'Depart from Me, you cursed, into the everlasting fire prepared for the devil and his angels:"

John 12:31 (NLT), "The time for judging this world has come, when Satan, the ruler of this world, will be cast out."

Although our enemy has power, his power is limited. He can only do what he is given permission to do. This means that although he is the prince of this world, he can only do what God allows him to do in this world. We see this in the story of Job. God stopped Satan and asked him what he was doing. When Satan told God that he came from walking up and down the earth, the Lord asked him had he considered his servant Job (Job 1:6-8). Satan then reminded God about the hedge of protection he had around Job that was preventing him from touching him. The Lord then told Satan "All right you may test him, . . . Do whatever you want with everything he possesses, but don't harm him physically." So, Satan left the LORD's presence" (Job 1:12).

Satan was only able to attack Job once he was given the permission to do so. But when God gave him permission, his attack could only go so far. It had to be within the guidelines given.

From the same passage of scripture, we see that Satan is not omnipresent. This means that he cannot be everywhere at the same time like God can. Because of this, he relies heavily on the demons, his angels that he oversees. This network of demons, at his direction, then walk around the earth fulfilling his assignments. They help with his attempts to nullify the effects of the Word of God. They also are the ones responsible for blinding people who do not believe, so they cannot understand the Gospel of Jesus Christ. And even further they are the ones that are behind tempting humans.

When Satan is not attacking and ordering attacks on believers, he's the one behind the accusations. According to Revelation 12:10 (NLT), *"Then I heard a loud voice shouting across the heavens, "It has come at last—salvation and power and the Kingdom of our God, and the authority of his Christ. For the accuser of our brothers and sisters has been thrown down to earth—the one who accuses them before our God day and night."* He loves going before God to list off the sins that we have committed. He does this because he hates the fact that believers are given many chances to repent when he wasn't.

When Satan is not making accusations, he's lying. According to John 8:44 (NLT), *"For you are the children of your father the devil, and you love to do the evil things he does. He was a murderer from the beginning. He has always hated the truth, because there is no truth in him. When he lies, it is consistent with his character; for he is a liar and the father of lies."* With his deception he blinds people and has them walking in disbelief, doubt and fear.

2 Corinthians 4:4 (NLT), "Satan, who is the god of this world, has blinded the minds of those who don't believe. They are unable to see the glorious light of the Good News. They don't understand this message about the glory of Christ, who is the exact likeness of God."

B. MANKIND'S POWER

Without the indwelling of the Holy Spirit, humans are powerless against the kingdom of darkness. According to

Hebrews 2:7-9 (NLT), *"Yet for a little while you made them a little lower than the angels and crowned them with glory and honor. You gave them authority over all things." Now when it says "all things," it means nothing is left out. But we have not yet seen all things put under their authority. What we see is Jesus, who for a little while was given a position "a little lower than angels"; and because he suffered death for us, he is now "crowned with glory and honor." Yes, by God's grace, Jesus tasted death for everyone."*
We are told from these passages of scripture that when Jesus took on the form of man, he became a little lower than the angels for the span of time he was on this earth. This scripture implies that once human, Jesus was lower in his nature and his condition. What we can take from this is that humans are lower than angels which means that we are not equal to or possess the same power that they possess.

Angels possess so much power, that they protect humans. In Psalm 91:11-13 we are told, *"For he will order angels to protect you wherever you go. 12 They will hold you up with their hands, so you won't even hurt your foot on a stone. 13 You will trample upon lions and cobras; you will crush fierce lions and serpents under your feet."*

As I mentioned previously, Satan once was one of the highest ranked angels in Heaven. When he was cast out of Heaven, his power wasn't diminished. Because of this, he and his angels are more powerful than humans. This is why without the indwelling and empowering of the Holy Spirit, we cannot do anything to defeat him.

C. HOLY SPIRIT'S UNLIMITED POWER

Believers are only capable of being able to resist the enemy when they have been given power to do so. This power is only given to believers by God. In Luke 10:19 (NKJV), prior to Jesus sending seventy labors out to spread the gospel, he said, "Behold, I give you the authority to trample on serpents and scorpions, and over all the power of the enemy, and nothing shall by any means hurt you."

Just like Jesus gave the seventy all power over the enemy back then, He is still doing it now through the Holy Spirit.

The Holy Spirit is the one who gives us the ability to resist the devil as well as all of those who are a part of the kingdom of darkness. The Holy Spirit is given to believers to dwell within them.

RESIST

Luke 11:13 (NLT), "So if you sinful people know how to give good gifts to your children, how much more will your heavenly Father give the Holy Spirit to those who ask him."

John 14:26 (NLT), "But when the Father sends the Advocate as my representative—that is, the Holy Spirit—he will teach you everything and will remind you of everything I have told you."

Romans 8:26 (NLT), "And the Holy Spirit helps us in our weakness..."

Acts 1:8 (NLT), "But you will receive power when the Holy Spirit comes upon you..."

1 Corinthians 6: 19 (NLT), "Don't you realize that your body is the temple of the Holy Spirit, who lives in you and was given to you by God? You do not belong to yourself."

Galatians 5:16 (NLT), "So I say, let the Holy Spirit guide your lives. Then you won't be doing what your sinful nature craves."

The Holy Spirit is extremely powerful because He is God's Spirit and Jesus' Spirit that dwells within us.

Romans 8:9 (NLT), "But you are not controlled by your sinful nature. You are controlled by the Spirit if you have the Spirit of God living in you. (And remember that those who do not have the Spirit of Christ living in them do not belong to him at all.)"

1 Corinthians 3:16, "Don't you realize that all of you together are the temple of God and that the Spirit of God lives in you?"

John 16:7 (NLT), "But in fact, it is best for you that I go away, because if I don't, the Advocate won't come. If I do go away, then I will send him to you."

John 15:26 (NLT), "But I will send you the Advocate—the Spirit of truth. He will come to you from the Father and will testify all about me."

John 14:16-20 (NLT), "And I will ask the Father, and he will give you another Advocate, who will never leave you. 17 HE is the Holy Spirit, who leads into all truth. The world cannot receive him, because it isn't looking for him and doesn't recognize him. But you know him, because he lives with you now and later will be in you. 18 No, I will not abandon you as orphans—I will come to you. 19 Soon the world will no longer see me, but you will see me. Since I live, you also will live. 20 When I am raised to life again, you will know that I am in my Father, and you are in me, and I am in you."

II. CAN THIS BE AVOIDED?

It does not matter how much we try to avoid being attacked by the enemy, we won't be able to. This is because, "...everyone who wants to live a godly life in Christ Jesus will suffer persecution" (2 Timothy 3:12 NLT). By definition persecution means, "to harass or punish in a manner designed to injure, grieve, or afflict. Or to annoy with persistent or urgent approaches (such as attacks, pleas, or opportunities)." What this means is that simply having a desire to live for Jesus Christ will cause you to become a target for the kingdom of darkness. The enemy will use whoever is available for him to use to attack you.

Although we cannot avoid the attacks of the enemy and those in the kingdom of darkness, we can resist their attacks. We do this by obeying the leading of the Holy Spirit. By staying alert, by watching out, because the devil is always prowling around like a roaring lion, looking for someone to devour (1 Peter 5:8). And we do this by fighting with the tools provided to us by the Lord.

A. YOU MUST FIGHT BECAUSE YOU SIGNED UP FOR THIS

Everyone who receives salvation is automatically enlisted as a soldier in the army of the Lord. Because of this, you are thrust into a battle with the enemy of the Lord: the kingdom of darkness. Once someone accepts Jesus Christ as their Lord and Savior, the devil becomes frustrated. His frustration causes you to now become his primary target, even though you may not have done any works for Christ yet. The mere fact that you confessed and received salvation was enough. Why? Because you made the decision to abandon living for the kingdom of darkness to now living for the Kingdom of God.

When you received salvation, you renounced your membership in the devil's army to become alive and a soldier in the Lord's army! Before you received salvation, even if you did not say that you worshiped or served the devil, you did just by walking in the flesh and fulfilling its desires. There is no in-between. It's either you live for and serve the kingdom of darkness, or the Kingdom of God.

Once the decision is made to live for the Lord, you go through an instant transformation where you are now restored to life. You literally take on the image of Christ, which in turn means that you now have the image of God again, and not the polluted sinful image of Adam.

Romans 8:29 (NKJV), "For whom He foreknew, He also predestined to be conformed to the image of His Son, that He might be the firstborn among many brethren."

2 Corinthians 3:18 (NKJV), "But we all, with unveiled face, beholding as in a mirror the glory of the Lord, are being transformed into the same image from glory to glory, just as by the Spirit of the Lord."

Romans 5:12 (NKJV), "Therefore, just as through one man sin entered the world, and death through sin, and thus death spread to all men, because all sinned---"

Romans 5:15-19(NLT), "But there is a great difference between Adam's sin and God's gracious gift. For the sin of this one man, Adam, brought death to many. But even greater is God's wonderful grace and his gift of forgiveness to many through this other man, Jesus Christ. 16 And the result of God's gracious gift is very different from the result of that one man's sin. For Adam's sin led to condemnation, but God's free gift leads to our being made right with God, even though we are guilty of many sins. 17 For the sin of this one man, Adam, caused death to rule over many. But even greater is God's wonderful grace and his gift of righteousness, for all who receive it will live in triumph over sin and death through this one man, Jesus Christ. 18 Yes, Adam's one sin brings condemnation for everyone, but Christ's one act of righteousness brings a right relationship with God and new life for everyone. Because one person disobeyed God, many became sinners. But because one other person obeyed God, many will be made righteous."

The fact that believers are image bearers of Christ is a driving force behind the constant attacks. Remember from the previous section that the devil wanted to be above God so badly that he came up with a detailed plan on what he was going to do to achieve it. However, instead of accomplishing his plan, the devil was thrown out of heaven. As a result of this, every time he sees the believer he is reminded of this defeat. He's reminded of the fact that he wasn't shown grace and mercy like the believer. Instead, he was cast out.

But that isn't all. When the devil looks at believers, he's reminded of the defeat that took place because of what Jesus did on the cross.

2 Timothy 3:16, 17 (NKJV), "All Scripture is given by inspiration of God, and is profitable for doctrine, for reproof, for correction, for instruction in righteousness, 17 that the man of God may be complete, thoroughly equipped for every go work."

B. WHAT DID JESUS' DEATH ON THE CROSS DO

When Jesus was crucified on the cross, the devil thought that he had finally won the battle against God. Little did he know that Jesus' death was not only the fulfillment of God's plan, but it would result in victory!

The fact that Jesus died meant that He now gained victory over death and sin once and for all. His death meant that mankind could be redeemed and restored back to their rightful position with God.

Revelation 1: 18 (NLT), "I am the living one. I died, but look—I am alive forever and ever! And I hold the keys of death and the grave."

1 Corinthians 15:55-57 (NLT), "O death, where is your victory? O death where is your sting?" 56 For sin is the sting that results in death and the law gives sin its power. 57 But thank God! He gives us victory over sin and death through our Lord Jesus Christ.

Romans 6:14 (NLT), "Sin is no longer your master, for you no longer live under the requirements of the law. Instead, you live under the freedom of God's grace."

Romans 6:23 (NLT), "For the wages of sin is death, but the free gift of God is eternal life through Christ Jesus our Lord."

RESIST

2 Timothy 1:10 (NLT), "And now he has made all of this plain to us by the appearing of Christ Jesus, our Savior. He broke the power of death and illuminated the way of life and immortality through the Good News."

Hebrews 2:14 (NLT), "Because God's children are human beings—made of flesh and blood—the Son also became flesh and blood. For only as a human being could he die, and only by dying could he break the power of the devil, who had the power of death."

1 Peter 2:24 (NLT), "He personally carried our sins in his body on the cross so that we can be dead to sin and live for what is right. By his wounds you are healed."

2 Corinthians 5:21 (NLT), "For God made Christ, who never sinned, to be the offering for our sin, so that we could be made right with God through Christ."

Because of Jesus' victory being transferred to believers, we don't have to fight for the victory. Rather, when we allow the Holy

Spirit to lead and guide us, and we wear the armor of God, we fight from a place of victory. Why? Because the victory of every battle that we will encounter on our journey was secured by the work that was done on the cross by Jesus.

Although the victory has already been secured by Jesus, every believer must still decide whether they will resist the devil and fight from a place or victory, or whether they will run in defeat. Not only
must this decision be made, but the decision of which weapons, strategies, and tactics that will be used must be made as well.

C. THE BATTLE

Soldiers who are in the army of the Lord, much like military soldiers, must also be prepared, and are also provided with strategy and tactics to assist them in times of warfare. Believers, regardless of position, title, or age in the kingdom, must be prepared to fight the devil, survive, and accomplish whatever is needed. They too are trained through policy and procedure: the Bible. And by engaging in actual battles. The weapons provided by God do not become outdated or ineffective. They never lose their power and are always the only weapons powerful enough to defeat the enemy.

When we find ourselves in a battle with the kingdom of darkness, if we are to be successful, we must do several things. The very first thing we must do is welcome the Holy Spirit to dwell within us. The Holy Spirit is a free gift from God. Which is given to us simply by us asking God for Him. This gift is not based upon position in the Kingdom, or the length of time you've been serving God either. God's desire is for all of His children to be filled with the Holy Spirit.

Without the assistance of the Holy Spirit, who is the power source, we are incapable of defeating the enemy. Without the Holy Spirit, we do not stand a chance against the devil or the kingdom of darkness—no matter how much we fight.

Being given the Holy Spirit is not enough to be able to resist and defeat the kingdom of darkness. Every believer must obey the leading of the Holy Spirit. Why? The Holy Spirit is the one who knows what we should and shouldn't do, where we should and shouldn't go. He knows the plans of the enemy, as well as the plans that God has for everyone, because He knows the mind of God. He even knows what attacks will come our way before they even happen.

> *1 Corinthians 2:11 (NLT), "No one can know a person's thoughts except that person's own spirit, and no one can know God's thoughts except God's own Spirit."*

Therefore, the Holy Spirit only speaks the truth and that which is permitted for Him to speak. Because of this, He will not lead us astray. This is why it is very important for believers to obey His leading if one has the desire to truly defeat the enemy and live a victorious life.

After there has been a decision made to follow the leading of the Holy Spirit, then it is imperative that believers put on and keep on the armor of God in order to defeat the enemy.

III. THE ARMOR OF GOD

> *"A final word: Be strong in the Lord and in his mighty power. Put on all of God's armor so that you will be able to stand firm against all strategies of the devil."*
> *(Ephesians 6:10-11 NLT)*

God is more powerful than the kingdom of darkness. God can do the impossible. There is literally nothing too hard for God, this includes defeating the kingdom of darkness repeatedly. We literally can do and accomplish any and everything through His power!

1 Chronicles 29:11 (NLT), "Yours, O LORD, is the greatness, the power, the glory, the victory, and the majesty. Everything in the heavens and on earth is yours, O LORD, and this is your kingdom. We adore you as the one who is over all things."

Matthew 19:26 (NLT), "Jesus looked at them intently and said, Humanly speaking, it is impossible. But with God everything is possible."

2 Timothy 1:7 (KJV), "For God did not give us the spirit of fear; but of power, and of love, and of a sound mind."

Ephesians 3:20 (NLT), "Now all glory to God, who is able, through his mighty power at work within us, to accomplish infinitely more than we might ask or think."

Philippians 4:13 (NLT), "For I can do everything through Christ, who gives me strength."

Luke 10:19 (NLT), "Look, I have given you authority over all the power of the enemy, and you can walk among snakes and scorpions and crush them. Nothing will injure you."

When we decide to accept the power that God has given to us, we must also take upon us His armor so that we will be able to stand against, resist, and defeat our enemy. We cannot just merely put on the armor of God when it's convenient for us. And we cannot afford to take the pieces of the armor of God off because we will be left open for attack. What soldier prepares for combat and neglects to put on all of his or her protective gear? Or what soldiers says, "I know this has worked well in previous battles and has been proven to be error proof, but I'll put this one on instead?" None that I can think of. A wise soldier would put on exactly what has worked and will keep it on until they are in a place of safety.

It is imperative that humans make the decision to put on the armor of God, which is spiritual, instead of trying to fight the enemy with carnal means. "For we are not fighting against flesh-

and-blood enemies, but against evil rulers and authority of the unseen world, against mighty powers in this dark world, and against evil spirits in the heavenly places" (Ephesians 6:12 NLT). Because of this, if we are to be successful in our battle with the kingdom of darkness we must,

" . . . put on every piece of God's armor so you will be able to resist the enemy in the time of evil" (Ephesians 6:13 NLT). Doing so will result in you standing in victory after the battle is over!

Ephesians 6:14-19,
14 Stand therefore, having your loins girt about with truth, and having on the breastplate of righteousness...

15 And your feet shod with the preparation of the gospel of peace...

16 Above all, taking the shield of faith, wherewith ye shall be able to quench all the fiery darts of the wicked.

17 And the helmet of salvation, and the sword of the Spirit which is the word of God.

A. THE BELT OF TRUTH

> *"Stand therefore, having your loins girt about with truth"*
> *(Ephesians 6:14)*

Without truth, it is impossible to stand against the plots, plans, schemes, and attacks of the devil. Therefore, we must be sure that we know what the truth is. The belt of truth has to do with the truth concerning Jesus Christ. Without the belt of truth, the other pieces of the armor of God would be to no effect.

According to John 14: 6, "Jesus is the way, the truth, and the life." It is only through Jesus Christ that we are able to come to God. There is no other way! This truth is important because it sets believers free. It also shines the light on the deception of the enemy.

Without being rooted and grounded in the truth of who Jesus is, what Jesus has done, the truth pertaining to the Word of God, as well as who we are in Jesus Christ, there is absolutely no way anyone will be able to defeat the enemy when we are engaged in warfare with him.

B. THE BREASTPLATE OF RIGHTEOUSNESS

"...and having on the breastplate of righteousness;"
(Ephesians 6:14 KJV)

A Roman or Israelite soldier wore a breastplate made of bronze or chain mail. The breastplate was, and still is, important because it covers the soldier's heart and lungs.

The breastplate for the believer refers to the righteousness that was purchased by Jesus Christ on the cross. This righteousness could not be obtained by humans because of our sinful nature. According to the King James Dictionary, Righteousness is, "Purity of heart and rectitude of life; conformity of heart and life to the divine law. . . The active and passive obedience of Christ, by which the law of God is fulfilled." The Bible's standard of human righteousness is God's own perfection in every area.

Even though we do not have the ability to achieve righteousness on our own, believers possess the righteousness of Christ. On the cross, Jesus exchanged our sin for His perfect righteousness. This exchange resulted in us being made righteous in the sight of God. We are literally accepted and treated as being in the right standing with God.

Romans 3:22 (NLT), "We are made right with God by placing our faith in Jesus Christ. And this is true for everyone who believes, no matter who we are."

2 Corinthians 5:21 (NLT), "For God made Christ, who never sinned, to be the offering for our sin, so that we could be made right with God through Christ."

Romans 3:10 (NLT), "As the Scriptures say, 'No one is righteous—not even one."

Once a believer receives salvation, a breastplate is issued to them. It's designed to protect the heart and soul from the deception and evil of the enemy. This breastplate is stamped with Jesus Christ's righteousness.

Romans 10:4 (NLT), "For Christ has already accomplished the purpose for which the law was given. As a result, all who believe in him are made right with God."

Although our breastplate is stamped with Jesus' righteousness, every believer must make righteous decisions to remain in right standing with God. According to Matthew 6:33 (NKJV), "But seek first the kingdom of God and His righteousness . . ." This lets us know that although we are covered with righteousness because of Jesus Christ, we must still work towards righteousness.

2 Timothy 2:22 (NLT), "Run from anything that stimulates youthful lusts. Instead pursue righteous living . . ."

Romans 1:17 (NLT), This Good News tells us how God makes us right in his sight. This is accomplished from start to finish by faith. As the Scriptures say, "It is through faith that a righteous person has life."

The breastplate of righteousness helps us to develop a heart of purity. It's important that our hearts are protected because it is the place where ill intentions flow. It's one of the places where the enemy likes to plant stuff.

Proverbs 4:23 (NLT), "Guard your heart above all else, for it determines the course of your life."

Mark 7:15 (NLT), "It's not what goes into your body that defiles you; you are defiled by what comes from your heart."

John 13:3 (NKJV), "And supper being ended, the devil having already put it into the heart of Judas Iscariot, Simon's son, to betray Him."

Acts 5:3 (NKJV), "But Peter said, "Ananias, why has Satan filled your heart to lie to the Holy Spirit and keep back part of the price of the kind for yourself?"

When we are focused on developing a pure heart, we are more likely to conform to the image of Christ. When we wear it, our choices become more righteous. These choices will in turn protect us from the deception of the enemy and temptation.

RESIST

Psalm 23: 3 (KJV), "He restoreth my soul: he leadeth me in the paths of righteousness for his name's sake."

How To Work Towards Being Righteous

When the Holy Spirit reveals an area in our lives that we must change, we must obey Him. We must allow Him to work through us. When we refuse to allow the Holy Spirit to work within us, it opens the door for Satan to come in and pull us away from being in right standing with God.

In our pursuit of righteousness, we must become a student of God's Word. Why? Because the Word of God is what leads and guides us in righteousness. It tells us what God requires. It also allows us to see what Jesus Christ did while He was here on earth.

Psalm 119:105 (NLT), "Your word is a lamp to guide my feet and a light for my path."

C. THE SHOES OF THE GOSPEL OF PEACE

"For shoes, put on the peace that comes from the Good News so that you will be fully prepared."
(Ephesians 6:15)

During training, a Roman soldier's shoes weren't like the combat boots that modern soldiers wear. Rather, they were studded with nails and spikes. They were similar to cleats. Their shoes helped them to keep their balance as they stood fighting against their enemy.

Like the shoes worn by the Roman soldier, the shoes that are worn by believers also help us to keep our balance as well. The gospel of peace is the message that Jesus gave to all of those who truly trust and believe in Him. It's the message that brings peace. It's also the message that prepares us for battle.

Our shoes help us to remain in our position in Christ by standing firm in the truth of God's word regardless of how difficult our battle with the enemy may be. These shoes help us to hold onto our faith no matter what. As well as confess Jesus Christ in difficult circumstances.

D. THE SHIELD OF FAITH

"In addition to all of these, hold up the shield of faith to stop the fiery arrows of the devil."
(Epehsians 6:16)

The shield was an important piece of the Roman soldier's military uniform. It is the first barrier which they possessed against their enemy's attack. During that time, their shield was used in all circumstances. Because of this, it was never left behind even though it was as large as a door and covered the soldier.

The Roman soldier used his shield in a defensive and offensive way. For example, it was used defensively to ward off the attacks of the enemy. It was also used offensively to push their enemy away from them. It was used to protect them from the arrows that were launched from their enemy. Because it was made of wood and covered in hide, the soldier was able to easily extinguish flaming arrows as well.

Just as the Roman soldier's shield was important for them, especially in protecting them from their enemy's arrows, the shield of faith is extremely important for believers. One of the greatest tactics of our enemy is to try to deceive us into doubting God. He does this because he knows that a believer having faith in God is of importance. He knows that without faith believers cannot please God!

Hebrews 11: 1 (NKJV), "Now faith is the substance of things hoped for, the evidence of things not seen."

Hebrews 11:6 (NKJV), "But without faith it is impossible to please Him, for he who comes to God must believe that He is, and that HE is a rewarder of those who diligently seek Him."

1 Corinthians 5:7(NKJV), "For we walk by faith, not by sight."

The enemy attacks our faith because he knows that it is a means by which we receive grace and enter into a relationship with God. He also knows that if we have faith, we will have hope in any situation, no matter how difficult it may appear to be.

Ephesians 2:8-9 (NLT), "God saved you by his grace when you believed. And you can't take credit for this; it is a gift from God. 9 Salvation is not a reward for the good things we have done, so none of us can boast about it."

Romans 5:1 (NLT), "Therefore, since we have been made right in God's sight by faith, we have peace with God because of what Jesus Christ our Lord has done for us."

Romans 5:2 (NLT), "Because of our faith, Christ has brought us into this place of undeserved privilege where we now stand, and we confidently and joyfully look forward to sharing God's glory."

Faith is what protects a believer and serves as a barrier between them and the attacks of the enemy. When a believer remains grounded in faith no matter how a situation looks, one is able to stand against the enemy and his schemes, plots and plans. And more importantly, one is able to extinguish the enemy's arrows.

E. THE HELMET OF SALVATION

"Put on salvation as your helmet..."
(Ephesians 6:17)

Historically, when a soldier suits up for battle, the last part of their uniform they put on is their helmet. The helmet is a very vital piece of a soldier's armor because it protects the head which houses the brain. It's very important to protect the head because the brain is the command station for the entire body. Without the head, the other parts of the body would be useless, and so would the other pieces of the soldier's armor.

Just like the helmet of the soldiers is an important part of their uniform, the helmet of salvation of the believer is also important. Salvation means to be delivered from our sins and the harmful consequences that come along with them. Jesus Christ already paid the ultimate price when he was crucified on the cross so that believers will have eternal life if they believe in Him.

John 3:16 (NLT), "For this is how God loved the world: He gave his one and only Son, so that everyone who believes in him will not perish but have eternal life."

John 14: 16 (NLT), "Jesus told him, I am the way, the truth, and the life. No one can come to the Father except through me."

Mark 16:16 (NLT), "Anyone who believes and is baptized will be saved. But anyone who refuses to believe will be condemned."

Romans 10:9 (NLT), "If you openly declare that Jesus is Lord and believe in your heart that God raised him from the dead, you will be saved."

Acts 4:12 (NLT), "There is salvation in no one else! God has given no other name under heaven by which we must be saved."

This means that salvation cannot be obtained by works. Rather, it is a free gift given to believers who believe in God.

Romans 6:23 (NLT), "For the wages of sin is death, but the free gift of God is eternal life through Christ Jesus our Lord."

Ephesians 2:8 (KJV), "For by grace are ye saved through faith; and that not of yourselves: it is the gift of God:"

The assurance of salvation is our greatest defense against anything the enemy throws at us. The helmet of salvation protects our minds. This is why we must grab a hold of our helmet and refuse to let go no matter how much the enemy tries to convince us otherwise.

The enemy's attack against the believer is focused on trying to convince the believer that they are not truly saved. He wants believers to believe that salvation can be easily lost. He wants us to believe that salvation is not limited to a one-time act. He does not want us to believe that salvation is continuous because of that which was done on the cross. He doesn't want us to hold fast to the truth that God's salvation is an ongoing, eternal state that believers enjoy.

Titus 3:5 (NLT), "...he saved us, not because of the righteous things we had done, but because of his mercy. He washed away our sins, giving us a new birth and new life through the Holy Spirit."

John 5:24 (NLT), "I tell you the truth, those who listen to my message and believe in God who sent me have eternal life. They will never be condemned for their sins, but they have already passed from death into life."

The enemy attempts to blind us in regard to salvation because he doesn't want us to truly understand that because of what was done on the cross he no longer has a hold on us! He doesn't want us to come into the knowledge that Jesus' death on the cross defeated the power of sin. And because of this defeat, believers have the power over sin when they allow Jesus Christ to lead them.

Romans 6:10 (NLT), "When he died, he died once to break the power sin. But now that he lives, he lives for the glory of God."

Romans 8:2 (NLT), "And because you belong to him, the power of the life-giving Spirit has freed you from the power of sin that leads to death."

1 Corinthians 1:18 (NLT), "The message of the cross is foolish to those who are headed for destruction! But we who are being saved know it is the very power of God."

The helmet of salvation helps us to prevent his fiery darts and arrows (lies) from being lodged into our minds. It does this by enabling us to destroy the lies, arguments, and opinions thrown at us by him. In essence, when we put on the helmet of salvation, we are better able to avoid and take control of sinful thoughts. We are able to discern what thoughts are good and true.

2 Corinthians 10:5 (KJV), "Casting down imaginations, and every high thing that exalteth itself against the knowledge of God, and bringing into captivity every thought to the obedience of Christ;"

Romans 12:2 (NLT), "Don't copy the behavior and customs of this world, but let God transform you into a new person by changing the way you think. Then you will learn to know God's will for you, which is good and pleasing and perfect."

How To Keep On The Helmet of Salvation

1. **Renew your mind:** One irrefutable fact is that our mind is a battlefield. This is why the enemy launches continuous attacks against it. Remember, if it's not protected, all other pieces of the armor are unless. Therefore, we must renew our minds by allowing the truth of God's word to take root and expose, wipe out, and uproot anything that is not supposed to be there or is contrary to it. We must allow it to wipe away old faulty ideas, opinions that are erroneous and contrary, worldly views, filthy lies, and confusion. It is imperative that we allow God's truth to take their place.

2. **Reject:** All thoughts and anything and everything that is against God's Word. This means that things like doubt, fear and disbelief must go immediately.

Psalm 55:22 (NLT), "Give your burdens to the LORD, and he will take care of you. He will not permit the godly to slip and fall."

2 Timothy 1:7 (NKJV), "For God has not given us a spirit of fear, but of power and of love and of a sound mind."

Philippians 4:6-7 (NLT), "Don't worry about anything; instead, pray about everything. Tell God what you need, and thank him for all he has done. 7 Then you will experience God's peace, which exceeds anything we can understand. His peace will guard your hearts and minds as you live in Christ Jesus."

1 Peter 5:7 (NLT), "Give all your worries and cares to God, for he cares about you."

3. **Look Up:** We must keep our eyes on Heaven. We must always remember our salvation and focus on eternity because our circumstances here on earth are not forever.

Hebrews 12:12 (NLT), "WE do this by keeping our eyes on Jesus, the champion who initiates and perfects our faith. Because of the joy awaiting him, he endured the cross, disregarding its shame, now he is seated in the place of honor beside God's throne."

Ephesians 2:6 (NLT), "For he raised us from the dead along with Christ and seated us with him in the heavenly realms because we are united with Christ Jesus."

Philippians 4:8 (NLT), "And now, dear brothers and sisters, one final thing. Fix your thoughts on what is true, and honorable, and right, and pure, and lovely, and admirable. Think about things that are excellent and worthy of praise."

4. **Remember victory was already won by Jesus:** There is no battle that you cannot win because Jesus already won them all! Therefore, whatever battle you may face, you're able to win it.

1 John 5:4 (KJV), "For whatsoever is born of God overcometh the world: and this is the victory that overcometh the world, even our faith."

1 John 4:4 (NLT), "But you belong to God, my dear children. You have already won a victory over those people, because the

Spirit who lives in you is greater than the spirit who lives in the world."

Colossians 2:15 (NKJV), "Having disarmed principalities and powers, He made a public spectacle of them, triumphing over them in it."

Revelations 12:11 (NLT), "And they have defeated him by the blood of the Lamb and by their testimony..."

5. **Take pride in and treasure salvation:** Always remember what salvation represents. Never forget the sacrifices made on the cross by Jesus Christ.

F. THE SWORD OF THE SPIRIT

"...and take the sword of the Spirit, which is the word of God." (Epehesians 6:17)

The sword used by Roman soldiers is both an offensive and defense weapon. It's used to protect one from harm or to do harm to an enemy. To ensure that the sword does what it is created to do, it is extremely imperative that the soldier who will be using it is trained prior to engaging in warfare.

Just as the Roman soldiers used a sword offensively and defensively against their enemy, believers do the same. The only difference is that the sword used by believers is the Word of God. This sword, just like that of the Roman soldier, is extremely important in protecting the believer and harming the enemy. Because of this, a believer must also be trained on how to use it prior to engaging in warfare with the enemy if there is going to be success.

The Sword of the Spirit is a two-edged sword that penetrates. It also cuts. And it is a discerner of truth. It reaches the heart and exposes motives and feelings as well. It helps us to demolish the strongholds of error and falsehood.

The Sword of the Spirit helps believers by providing strength. It also helps believers to withstand the attacks of Satan. The more that believers know and live the Word of God, the more effective they are against the enemy!

Hebrews 4:12 (NLT), "For the word of God is alive and powerful. It is sharper than the sharpest two-edged sword, cutting between soul and spirit, between joint and marrow. It exposes our innermost thoughts and desires."

2 Timothy 3:16-17 (NLT), "All Scripture is inspired by God and is useful to teach us what is true and to make us realize what is wrong in our lives. It corrects us when we are wrong and teaches us to do what is right. 17 God uses it to prepare and equip his people to do every good work."

2 Corinthians 10:4-5 (NLT), "We use God's mighty weapons, not worldly weapons, to knock down the strongholds of human reasoning and to destroy false arguments. 5 We destroy every proud obstacle that keeps people from knowing God. We capture their rebellious thoughts and teach them to obey Christ."

Psalm 119:11 (NLT), "I have hidden your word in my heart, that I might not sin against you."

In conclusion, the armor of God, when worn and not taken off, is one of the most powerful undefeated weapons given to mankind by God.

FLEE

III

FLEE

By definition to flee means, "to run away from a place or situation of danger." Or, "to run away often from danger or evil." A situation which began as a result of an attack initiated by the enemy (the rulers of darkness of this world and spiritual wickedness) will end as a result of your submission, your decision to use the power given to you, and fighting with the armor of God. The kingdom of darkness will run away from you because of the dangerous situation created. Did you catch that? Whenever you stand firm and exert the power that the Lord has given to you and suit up and stay suited up the enemy will run away from you, and you will still be standing no matter how battered or bruised you are. You win!

You'll literally obtain victory over the one that, "...prowls around like a roaring lion, looking for someone to devour" (1 Peter 5:8 NLT). You will defeat the one that is, "...a murderer from the beginning of time" (John 8:44 NLT). You'll overtake the thief whose, "...purpose is to steal and kill and destroy; and "...the commander of the power in the unseen world..."

Your enemy will flee because he, and the other evil spirits that make up the kingdom of darkness, know that they don't stand a chance against a believer that stands in a place of authority and fights with spiritual means. He knows that no matter what he tries to do, he is a defeated foe and lacks the ability to obtain the victory.

Although the enemy will flee, please be mindful that he will come back again when he is granted permission by God. He'll watch and wait for the perfect opportunity too. During that time, he'll be studying you and looking for your weakness. He'll also be releasing accusations against you to God.

This is why you must remain alert, sober minded, and ready to battle once again.

THE IMPORTANCE OF PRAYER

IV
THE IMPORTANCE OF PRAYER

"Pray in the Spirit at all times and on every occasion..."
(Ephesians 6:19)

Although prayer is not a piece of the armor of God, it is still important and should be done if we are to submit to God and resist the enemy. Why? Because prayer is one avenue that God uses to communicate His desires, instructions, and insight to us. Without prayer, believers would not know the voice of God and will be led astray by the enemy.

What is Prayer

Prayer is communication between you and God. It occurs when you talk to Him. And when you listen for His response. It is the primary way that you communicate your thoughts and desires to God. It is the way that you make requests to Him.

Prayer is something that cannot be neglected. Prayer, especially when done on a regular basis, facilitates intimacy. Which in turn will result in a strong relationship with God.

Although there are several types of prayers, the one that is important when resisting our enemy is the prayer of supplication. The prayer of supplication involves making a request to God on your own behalf. As you are engaged in warfare with the enemy, it is imperative that you ask God things, request direction, vision, and strategy if you are to succeed!

1 Thessalonians 5:17(NLT), "Never stop praying."

John 15:7 (NLT), "But if you remain in me and my words remain in you, you may ask for anything you want, and it will be granted."

THE IMPORTANCE OF PRAYER

Philippians 4:6-7 (NLT), "Don't worry about anything; instead, pray about everything. Tell God what you need, and thank him for all he has done. 7 Then you will experience God's peace, which exceeds anything we can understand. His peace will guard your hearts and minds as you live in Christ Jesus."

1 John 5:14 (NLT), "And we are confident that he hears us whenever we ask for anything that pleases him."

THOSE WHO SUBMITTED AND RESISTED

V

THOSE WHO SUBMITTED AND RESISTED

JOB: THE PERFECT AND UPRIGHT MAN

Job 1:1 (NLT), "There once was a man named Job who lived in the land of Uz. He was blameless—a man of complete integrity. He feared God and stayed away from evil."

Job was a man that lived for God. He was considered perfect because he, unlike his 10 children and others, stayed away from evil. Job was considered the richest man in that area because he had seven thousand sheep, three thousand camels, five hundred teams of oxen, and 500 female donkeys (Job 1:2).

Although Job had been living for God, he was not exempt from suffering and from being attacked by the enemy. In fact, God is the one who suggested that the enemy test Job. According to Job 1:6 (NLT), "One day the members of the heavenly court came to present themselves before the LORD, and the Accuser, Satan, came with them." The Lord then asked Satan where he had come from. Satan replied, "I have been patrolling the earth, watching everything that's going on" (Job 1:7). It was after this comment that the Lord asked Satan, "Have you noticed my servant Job? He is the finest man in all the earth. He is blameless—a man of complete integrity. He fears God and stays away from evil" (Job 1:8).

After conversing further, the Lord gave Satan permission to test Job. He said to Satan, "Do whatever you want with everything he possesses, but don't harm him physically (Job 1:12 NLT). So, Satan left God's presence with the authority he had been given. Satan did not waste time in exercising that authority. He caused several events to happen that resulted in the loss of all of Job's livestock as well as his children.

Job's response when he had been tempted and tried by the devil was remarkable. Despite his pain and loss, he kept on the armor that God had given him. Job did not complain. Job did not turn

THOSE WHO SUBMITTED AND RESISTED

away from God either. According to Job 1:20-22 (NLT), *"Job stood up and tore his robe in grief. Then he shaved his head and fell to the ground to worship. 21 He said, 'I came naked from my mother's womb, and I will be naked when I leave. The Lord gave me what I had, and the Lord has taken it away. Praise the name of the Lord!' 22 In all of this, Job did not sin by blaming God."*

Although the enemy fled from Job, he did return a second time to tempt and try Job. He did this only because God had given him permission again. This time the enemy was allowed to touch his body. But not before the Lord said this: *"Have you noticed my servant Job? He is the finest man in all the earth. He is blameless— a man of complete integrity. He fears God and stays away from evil. And he has maintained his integrity, even though you urged me to harm him without cause"* (Job 2:3 NLT). This verse shows us two very important things. Even though the Lord initiates the interactions with the enemy by speaking highly of you, the enemy's desire is always to harm you. It also shows that God is watching during the attack. That's the only reason that God knew that Job had maintained his integrity.

Could it be that the attacks of the enemy are allowed in our lives in order for the Lord to show the enemy what we are made of? Or to pull what is inside of us out more? Or to give us more than we once had? I believe so because Job's faithfulness was rewarded by God in the end.

Job 42: 12- 13, 15 (NLT), "So the Lord blessed Job in the second half of his life even more than in the beginning. For now he had 14,000 sheep, 6,000 camels, 1,000 teams of oxen, and 1,000 female donkeys. 13 He also gave Job seven more sons and three more daughters."

Job 42:15 (NLT), "In all the land no women were as lovely as the daughters of Job. And their father put them into his will along with their brothers."

THE TAKEAWAY

James 4:7 was alive and active in Job's life. This is why he was able to defeat the enemy.

1. Job was already submitted to God. This is inferred by the fact that God called him, "the finest man in all the earth, blameless and a man with complete integrity who loves God and stays away from evil."

2. Job was able to resist the enemy's attack. The enemy told God that Job would curse Him to His face if all that he had was taken away (Job 1:11). When Job's property, children, and body was afflicted, he did not curse God. His first response was to worship God. Job's second response was to rebuke his wife by telling her, "You talk like a foolish woman. Should we accept only good things from the hand of God and never anything bad?" (Job 2:10 NLT). In saying that, he did not curse God as the enemy desired. And even though Job had weary moments and wanted to die because of the afflictions he had been experiencing, he continued to resist cursing God.

3. The enemy ultimately fled from Job: After each attack, the enemy had no other choice but to leave Job alone. The enemy could only go so far with Job. Because Job resisted and didn't curse God, the enemy's argument was proven to be wrong. He had no other choice but to flee because he was powerless against the man who remained blameless, who continued to love God throughout the battle, and whose integrity remained intact.

The Enemy's Attack Is Not Always Caused By Sin

Even when you find yourself being attacked by the enemy, you cannot automatically assume that it is because you have done something wrong, or that sin is present in your life. Remember, Job was considered by God to be a man that was blameless and with complete integrity. But God decided, in His infinite wisdom, to lower the hedge of protection He had placed around Job that had been protecting Job.

God set Job up for the attack because he was submitted to Him. It is my belief that God knew that Job would be able to resist the enemy despite the attacks because of his love for Him and Job's hatred of evil. God did this because He knew what he wanted to release to Job.

This is what happens with us. God gives the enemy permission to attack us. God knows that if we grab ahold of what was given to us to fight the enemy that we will still be standing in the end like Job.

Just A Little Encouragement

If you are currently going through a season where you feel as though you are in a constant fight, hold on. As long as you

THOSE WHO SUBMITTED AND RESISTED

continue to fight with what God has given you, the enemy will flee. Remember, you aren't fighting for the victory. Instead you are fighting from a place of victory awaiting the manifestation of what has already been won.

Romans 8:28 (NLT), "And we know that God causes everything to work together for the good of those who love God and are called according to his purpose for them."

1 Peter 5:10 (NLT), "In his kindness God called you to share in his eternal glory by means of Christ Jesus. So after you have suffered a little while, he will restore, support, and strengthen you, and he will place you on a firm foundation."

Hebrews 13:5 (NLT), "For God has said, "I will never fail you. I will never abandon you.""

JESUS: THE GREATEST EXAMPLE

It doesn't matter who you are or how long you've lived for Christ, the devil will launch attacks against you. It doesn't matter how many victories you have previously won against him either, he will still attack you hoping that he catches you off guard. Or he'll wait until he thinks you're vulnerable and at your weakest point and attack you in hopes of triumphing over you.

We see this very thing happening to Jesus, the living WORD! According to Luke 3: 21-22, Jesus, after being baptized by John the Baptist, and everyone seeing the light shining from Heaven, and hearing God say, *"this is my beloved Son who I am well pleased"* was led in the wilderness by the Holy Spirit to be tempted by the devil 40 days and 40 nights (Luke 4:1-2).

It was only after the 40 day and 40-night period, when Jesus was weak and hungry, that the devil came to tempt Him (Luke 4:2). According to Luke 4:3, the enemy told Jesus, *"If you are the Son of God, tell this stone to become a loaf of bread."* To which Jesus replied, *"No! The Scriptures say, 'People do not live by bread alone.'"* It was at this point that Jesus stood using the Sword of the Spirit against the enemy when he attempted to draw Jesus away by the lust of the flesh.

As Jesus continued to stand in position resisting the enemy, the enemy kept launching attacks against him. This time he tempted Jesus with the lust of the eyes. According to Luke 4:5-7, *"Then the devil took him up and revealed to him all the kingdoms of the world in a moment of time. 6 "I will give you the glory of these kingdoms and authority over them;" the devil said, "because they are mine to give to anyone I please. 7 I will give it all to you if you will worship me."* To which Jesus replied, *"The Scriptures say, 'You must worship the Lord your God and serve only him."* Again, Jesus resisted the enemy by continuing to use the armor of God.

But this still didn't stop the devil from trying to tempt Jesus a third time. The devil took Jesus to the highest point of the Temple in Jerusalem, and said, *"If you are the son of God, jump off! For the Scriptures say, 'He will order his angels to protect and guard you. And they will hold you up with their hands, so you won't even hurt your foot on a stone'"* (Luke 4:9-11 NLT). Instead of Jesus becoming emotional and throwing a fit because the enemy kept going after him, he simply continued to rely on the armor of God. Jesus replied, *"The Scriptures also say, 'You must not test the Lord your God'"* (Luke 4:12 NLT). After tempting Jesus for a third time and being resisted, the devil had no other choice but to flee another time.

Luke 4:13 (NLT), "When the devil had finished tempting Jesus, he left him until the next opportunity came."

Jesus was left standing after being tempted by the enemy because of Him wearing, relying on, and using the armor of God. Had He not believed in the truth of God's Word, He would have given into the enemy's trick when he twisted scripture. Had Jesus not worn the shoes of the gospel of peace, He would not have been able to stand firmly resisting the devil's back to back blows. Had he not had on the shield of faith, Jesus would have forfeited all that God had in store for Him for its counterfeit. Had Jesus not had on His helmet of salvation, the devil's deceptive seeds would have taken root and caused Him to doubt God. And lastly, had Jesus not known how to use the Sword of the Spirit, He would have failed miserably at cutting through the lies of the enemy when he misquoted scripture.

THE TAKEAWAY

If the devil was bold enough to launch attacks against our Lord and Savior, he will not hesitate to do the same to you! Even though He will, you can obtain the victory by standing firm and following the example that Jesus left for us in Luke 4:

THOSE WHO SUBMITTED AND RESISTED

1. Don't allow your own lusts to carry you away.
2. Continue to submit to and be led by the Holy Spirit.
3. Stand in a place of authority and use the greatest weapon that is available to you—the armor of God.

James 1:4 (NLT), "Temptation comes from our own desires, which entice us and drag us away."

1 Corinthians 10:13 (NLT), "The temptations in your life are no different from what others experience. And God is faithful. He will not allow the temptation to be more than you can stand. When you are tempted, he will show you a way out so that you can endure."

CONCLUSION

CONCLUSION

It does not matter how powerful and wicked the enemy may seem, you can still obtain victory over him and all of those who are a part of the kingdom of darkness. It's totally up to you! You must make the decision that you'll submit everything to the Lord. You must decide that you'll stand resisting the devil by fighting with the whole armor of God on. You must decide no matter how difficult the fight gets that you will stand and keep fighting. Then and only then will you be able to live a life filled with continuous victories.

Always remember, no matter how hard the battle, victory was already won for you on the cross by our Lord and Savior Jesus Christ . . .

ABOUT THE AUTHOR

Roszien Kay Lewis- Juris Doctor, speaker and entrepreneur- is an emerging leader and catalyst with a prophetic voice. She has a deep rooted desire to see people healed, delivered, and set free. As a result she founded Destined to Be Released Ministries, a ministry whose sole objective is to encourage, teach, and equip others through the Word of God. Roszien has hosted conferences, workshops, and spearheads the "21 Day Jump Start My Draw" prayer challenge.

As a result of the trauma she suffered in her childhood and teenage years, Roszien formed #ConfessionsOfAnOvercomer motivational speaking company. Through this company she shares her testimony of overcoming every obstacle in her life. And she encourages others that they too can overcome anything as long as they believe in themselves.

When Roszien is not ministering to or mentoring others, she's busy assisting others with book publishing. She is the sole owner of Confessions Publishing, a Christian based publishing company that assists authors with "turning their manuscripts into a masterpiece."

Roszien resides in California with her two beautiful daughters, Aaliyah and Myah.

CONTACT ROSZIEN

FACEBOOK: ROSZIEN KAY LEWIS

IG: ROSZIEN KAY LEWIS

EMAIL: roszien@gmail.com

www.ingramcontent.com/pod-product-compliance
Lightning Source LLC
LaVergne TN
LVHW041632070426
835507LV00008B/579